PETS UNDERCOVER!

The TRUTH About RABBITS

What Rabbits Do When You're Not Looking

MARY COLSON

raintree
a Capstone company — publishers for children

Raintree is an imprint of Capstone Global Library Limited, a company incorporated in England and Wales having its registered office at 264 Banbury Road, Oxford, OX2 7DY – Registered company number: 6695582

www.raintree.co.uk
myorders@raintree.co.uk

Edited by Helen Cox Cannons
Designed by Philippa Jenkins
Picture research by Morgan Walters
Production by Laura Manthe
Originated by Capstone Global Library Limited
Printed and bound in China

ISBN 978 1 4747 3852 1
21 20 19 18 17
10 9 8 7 6 5 4 3 2 1

British Library Cataloguing in Publication Data
A full catalogue record for this book is available from the British Library.

Acknowledgements
We would like to thank the following for permission to reproduce photographs: Alamy: Nature Picture Library, top 11; Capstone Studio: Karon Dubke, 5, 7, 9, 11, 13, 15, 17, 19, 21, 23, 25, 27, 29; iStockphoto: dirkvandevyver, (rabbit teeth) 21.

We would like to thank Ros Lamb from the Rabbit Welfare Association and Fund for her invaluable help in the preparation of this book.

Disclaimer
All the internet addresses (URLs) given in this book were valid at the time of going to press. However, due to the dynamic nature of the internet, some addresses may have changed, or sites may have changed or ceased to exist since publication. While the author and publishers regret any inconvenience this may cause readers, no responsibility for any such changes can be accepted by either the author or the publishers.

Some words are shown in bold, **like this**. You can find out what they mean by looking in the glossary.

Contents

Hello!

Well, hello there! Pleased to meet you! I'm Jemima. I live with Becca, Abby, Mum, Dad and my best friend, Bella. Bella is another rabbit. She keeps me company.

Everyone else is going out today. They are taking Bella to the vet. While they're away I'm going to have lots of fun. See that **glint** in my eye? Read on to find out how wild I really am!

Hoppity hop!

Bye, Bella – see you later!

When everyone goes out, I roam around the house. I'm full of energy in the mornings and evenings. In fact, I'm a hopping machine! My **hind legs** are super-strong. I push off from my big, long back paws. My **bobtail** wobbles when I hop!

Snacks and nibbles

Yum! I love breakfast time! My favourite foods are hay, grass and leafy green vegetables. I don't mind carrots, either. Please don't find this too gross, but I sometimes eat my own poo! I need to eat my poo to **digest** my food properly.

Leaping into action

I'm quite happy to sit and nibble at the moment, but you should see me **binky**! When rabbits binky, they run fast and jump in the air. They twist their bodies and flick their feet.

When I binky, it means that I'm *really* happy. I can jump over 1 metre (3.3 feet) high and 3 metres (9.8 feet) long!

That's my patch!

Don't even think of just walking in here! This is my **patch**, and I'm in charge. I rub my **scent** on everything.

Sniff! I smell things and then rub them with my chin. That's where my **scent glands** are. When people visit I sniff and rub them. Then when they visit again, I know they are friends.

Sensing danger

I can hear something. Who's there? I have good hearing and can hear the smallest noise. My twitching nose can pick up new smells. My whiskers sense movement nearby. I'm ready and waiting. Is this a friend or a **foe**? Oh, it's just the ice cream van coming along the road.

Staying out of trouble

My wild nature comes out if I sense danger. I stand on my **hind legs** to be taller. I warn my family that something is coming. If you see me thumping the ground with my foot, it's not because I'm tap dancing. My foot thumping is my code for danger. Run!

Running in zigzags

My eyes are on the sides of my head. This means I can see backwards and forwards. I can see danger creeping up from anywhere. If I need to make a quick getaway, I run in zigzags. This confuses the animal that's chasing me. When I do this, even Becca and Abby can't catch me!

Leave me alone!

I grind my teeth when I'm hopping mad! Becca and Abby have cleaned my **hutch** and **rearranged** my stuff. I don't like it, and I want it like it was. I might just grunt at them.

Rabbits can also charge and pound at other animals with their paws when they are really angry. But I'm too polite for that!

My way of keeping clean

I keep clean in different ways from you. My fur gets dirty so I lick it clean. I use my teeth to get the really big bits of dirt out.

My fur **sheds** sometimes. It's why I'm not allowed to sit on the sofa. (I do anyway, but please don't tell my family!)

Making a mark

My teeth never stop growing. I have to chew to keep them the right length. Chewing hay keeps them worn down, but I nibble anything – wires, chair legs, shoes, you name it. Oh, and Abby's shoes! Don't leave anything **precious** near me, or I will nibble it to shreds.

When you go to sleep...

Wheee! Round and round, I run! I have had some food, and I'm full of energy! I run in circles to show I want to play, but Becca, Abby and Bella have gone to sleep. After a final spin, I burrow down into my **hutch**. I need to get some sleep. After all, I've got another busy day tomorrow!

How wild is *your* rabbit?

1. What does your rabbit do to warn others of danger?

a) Its nose twitches and its ears stand up.

b) It runs around in circles.

c) It thumps the ground with its back feet like a drumroll!

2. What does your rabbit do to get away from danger?

a) It burrows down in its hutch.

b) It crouches down low and closes its eyes.

c) It races away, running fast in zigzags!

3. How do you know your rabbit is happy?

a) It chews on hay and grass.

b) It chases its own tail.

c) It runs and leaps in the air, flicking out its back legs!

4. What does your rabbit eat to get extra **nutrients**?

a) It eats lots of hay.

b) It snacks on spinach. (Well, it works for Popeye!)

c) It eats its own poo – ewww!

To find out how wild your rabbit is, check the results on page 32.

Glossary

binky high hop a rabbit might do when it is happy

bobtail short tail, such as the fluffy one a rabbit has

digest break down food so the body can get all the food's goodness

foe enemy

glint flash of light, shiny

hind legs back legs

hutch box or cage where a rabbit sleeps and rests

nutrients parts of food that the body needs for energy and good health

patch territory; area where something lives or roams

precious of great value; greatly loved

rearrange put in a different place or order

scent smell

scent glands special organs in the body that make smells

sheds falls out

Find out more

Books

Bunny's Guide to Caring for Your Rabbit (Pets' Guides), Anita Ganeri (Raintree, 2013)

Pet Rabbits: Questions and Answers (Pet Questions and Answers), Christina Mia Gardeski (Raintree, 2016)

Rabbits (Animal Family Albums), Charlotte Guillain (Raintree, 2013)

Websites

http://rabbitwelfare.co.uk/pdfs/ RWAbrochuremaster.pdf
This booklet gives lots of useful information on how to care for rabbits.

www.rspca.org.uk/adviceandwelfare/pets/ rabbits
This page on the RSPCA website is full of fascinating facts about rabbits and how to care for them.

Index

Quiz answers:

Mostly As: You have a very laid-back rabbit! It tries to be wild, but it's happier getting warm and cosy in its bed!

Mostly Bs: Your rabbit is pretty wild. It runs around a lot, but if danger comes, it looks the other way!

Mostly Cs: You own one really wild rabbit! It can hardly be controlled! It's a thumping, running, poo-eating wild thing!